A JOURNEY THROUGH

Emotions

ANGEL

authorHOUSE®

AuthorHouse™
1663 Liberty Drive
Bloomington, IN 47403
www.authorhouse.com
Phone: 1-800-839-8640

First published by AuthorHouse   11/29/2011

ISBN: 978-1-4678-7151-8 (sc)
ISBN: 978-1-4678-7150-1 (ebk)

Library of Congress Control Number: 2011960541

Printed in the United States of America

Any people depicted in stock imagery provided by Thinkstock are models, and such images are being used for illustrative purposes only.
Certain stock imagery © Thinkstock.

This book is printed on acid-free paper.

Contents

Spirit Lifting *1*

A Conversation 3
God Pulled Me Through 5
Dreams 6
Life 7
My Angel Calls 8
Who Am I 9
God Watches 11
A Soldiers Song 13

A Special kind of Love *15*

Friends Before Lovers 17
From Pain to Joy 19
A Mothers Gift 20
A Mothers' Love 22
The Legacy of A Matriarch 23
My Son, My blessing 25
My Child, My Gift 27
Daughter of My Heart 29

Illusions of Love Lost *31*

Love Gone Cold *33*
A Lonely Road *35*
Guilty Of Love *37*
Just an Illusion *38*
Happy to Let Em' Go *40*
Honesty *41*
I lied *42*
Broken Heart *43*
A Haunting Decision *44*
Hurting *46*

A Women's Worth *47*

Behind Closed Doors *49*
Foolish Pride *50*
Self Deception *52*
Know Thy Self *53*
Forgiveness *55*
I'am, I see, I know *57*
Standing Tall, Standing Proud *59*
Trust *60*
Searching for Love *61*

Life's Lessons and Trials *63*

Past, Present, and Future *65*
America's Shame *66*
My shame Vs My Pride *68*
Judgment . . . Who Are You *70*
Judgement . . . . Race Part 2 ....*71*

Life Pulls No Punches 73
Drug Dealer 74
Isn't It Ironic 75
Mirror Image 76
A Heavy Load 78
A Letter to a Drug Addict 79
Searching for Redemption 81
Worthy . . . Or Not 83
Contemplation 84
Is it Worth It 86
Essence of Life 87
Random Thoughts 89
Pondering Questions 90
This Too Shall Pass 91

Humorous 93

Momma Knows 95
Subject: Men 96
Loves Price 97

Saying Good-Bye 99

A Broken Promise 101
My Love, My Loss 102
Forget Not 103
Had I Only Known 105

Spirit Lifting

A Conversation

I had a conversation with the Lord the
other day, some things were on my mind so
I asked him these questions when
I prayed

Lord why are my skies so often dull and grey? He
answered" your skies are not so much grey as you may
seem to think, they are really a very light shade if blue"

Lord" I said why do you take some of the most warm
and kind people and leave this world so full of hatred
and evil?"

He replied "I take all of my children home at some
point and time in their life, when their work on this
earth is through, just as when the time is right and
your work for me is done your place is with me and my
home you too will come."

"Lord, why do I sometimes have these visions that I and only I can see? and why is it that when I do they are filled with tragedies I can't tell anyone ahead of time because I'm not sure if this will come to pass and don't want to look like a fool"

The Lord said "there are somethings in this universe that are not for you to understand, these visions you speak of, that to you seem tragic are given as warnings and will prepare you ahead of time and they too shall come to pass; that is all that I will say these are all the questions for today you may ask."

God Pulled Me Through

There are things that God has pulled me through, that
I cannot even imagine telling you

He has picked me up when I was down, he helped me
through the tough times when my so called friends
were nowhere to be
found

God has pulled me through so many things, I just wish
I could tell you but it's between him and me you see,
something special for
God and me.

Dreams

They are like the wind, some are strong and forceful
making you realize what it is that you really want
out of life while others are weak, drifting on a slight
summer breeze, you'd never know it was even there
until it has passed you by

They are always within your grasp all you have to do is
realize what they are and reach out and take control, no
dreams are dreamt too young and you can never grow
to old, too old to realize what your dreams are and
make them into a
reality.

Life

Life is like a river always flowing never ending, yet at
some point our life as we know it will end, however
life in general just keeps on flowing for when your life
comes to an end, another life will
begin.

Although the twists and turns that we will all go
through, nothing on this earth or even in this lifetime
can compare, come close to what God can and has
given to me and to you.

Life is full of decisions regarding right and wrong, the
choices that we make today that we ourselves think may
be right could in fact be terribly wrong, however we
must learn from the mistakes because life never stops
for us to catch up it just moves on and that's simply . . .

Life

My Angel Calls

Out of my darkest moments of despair or whenever I'm
thinking wicked thoughts, I look up and you are there
and through my tears I see your smiling face telling me
it will be alright now that you are here, you put a smile
back on my
face

Now out of the darkness and into the light, even when
I' think I may be wrong you tell me you know I'm
right, you keep me going when I want to stop, you tell
me I can do it, I can make it to the
top

From the top of the mountain . . . . My Angel Calls . . . .
Love you Papa C the Angel that answered Gods
final call . . .

Who Am I

Can you see me? Can you feel me?
Can you talk to me? Yes, yet you can not
Yet you know that I'm there, I see you, I see you very
clearly, I'm so in tune with your feelings that I feel your
happiness and pain, my touch is as light as a feather, my
presence as transparent as
the wind

Do you know who I am? Do you know what I am?

I am you in all your crowning glory, I am you in your
moments of despair, you even say you love me, you may
even be able to recite passages of my book, I am there
whenever you need me, by your side day and night, in
your head, but am I in
your heart?

Look inside your heart and see for you were made in the image of me, only you can find these answers

I know you inside and out but do you know who I am?

Who am I? Who am I to you?

Who Am I . . . .???

God Watches

He watches those who do to you wrong, so pay close
attention to what is said
in this poem

God saw what you did to me, you made my heart cry,
and my soul bleed, you made my dreams fall down at
your feet, while trampling me in defeat

I have forgiven you just like he told me to, it's just so
hard to believe I could let my heart be so deceived . . .

That fateful day I met you, I let God go and followed
you, letting you lead me in the wrong direction, like a
child I was starving for affection . . .

Following you led me to a life of poor stricken poverty,
a place in life I swore to never be, when you beat me
down, it was he who picked me up, he pat my head and
hit my butt, then he told me to try again, it was then I
knew that it was God who was
my true
friend . . .

God watches those who do you wrong, no matter what
you go through or how far away from him you stray,
when you return to him he will always find a place in
his home for
you to stay . . .

My dear don't turn God away, no matter how bleak
your out look in life may be, take your problems and
turn your life over to him, and he will give you peace
and eventually set you free . . .

God Watches

A Soldiers Song

You see I don't know you all personally, but I know
you're out there serving this country for me, no one
knows the heart it takes to do what you do for us day
after day, or the
thoughts you hide
inside . . .

I know that every day and night you're out there you
thank God for that one more day in your life that you
have
survived . . .

We owe you for the blood, the sweat, and all your tears,
all these have helped keep us safe as well year
after year . . .

Stars that shine so bright with a blinding light
represent the different states as well as the nationalities
who fight side by side putting away all differences
blending them together pledging allegiance under
one flag . . .

Red is for the blood in your veins that so many of you
have shed . . .
White is for the purity in your soul that runs deep with
a love for this for this country that makes me want to
weep,
Blue is for the bravery you show again and again, this
is why our flag rises so high and stands so true, you see
America would not be America if it were not for
all
of
you . . .

A Special kind of Love

Friends Before Lovers

One August day a boy and a girl were out at play that,
boy and girl were you and I, over the years we became
closer than friends as
you stole my heart away,
way back then . . .

Friends we were but somehow we drifted apart I had
to go away and that just tore at my fragile heart, you
found yourself a new girlfriend, you both showing up
as you did, that news broke my heart, my dreams were
shattered,
at an end, claiming that you did not know how much I
cared for you, but in my heart, of hearts I thought you
knew . . .

After a while you told me you were free, my heart felt
light and it was almost
like it use to be, as we cleared the air and got that
problem out the way, you seemed surprised at what I
had to say, which were . . .
I love you,
Three little words with a world of meaning,
That look in your eyes, it tells me that you have the
same feelings . . .

That boy and girl were friends back then, now he's my
lover,
my husband,
and also
my best friend

From Pain to Joy

There comes a time in everyone's life when it seems
that love will never find a place in their heart . . .

I was one of those people at one time, always the center
of attention yet inside I was feeling desolate, alone even
in a crowd I felt dead, empty like I had nothing left to
give of myself

Then one day I met you and when I looked into your
eyes I saw a kind and peaceful soul and it took me by
surprise . . . .

In a world so cold and at times even cruel, men with a
soul like yours are hard to find, you're like a jewel, and
yes it was all in your eyes,

It was at that moment, that single moment when I
knew that we would never part, I knew this because
it was then I gave to you my heart . . . My Husband,
Lover and Best Friend . . .

A Mothers Gift

I love you for the silent tears you've cried, the time that
you gave and all the sacrifices you've made, I love you
for the times you had to BEG, STEAL or BORROW,
just to make sure your children had a better chance
tomorrow . . .

Always there to comfort me when no one else could see
there was something wrong, you were there to wipe my
first tear and when I had my first fear, when my world
came crashing down and you saw this to be true, it was
YOU who rushed to pick me up off the ground letting
me know that GOD was still around . . .

There is so very much more that I could say, but
thinking about your silent strength just takes my
breath away, I want to thank you for all you for all that
you've done and to remind you that you are the one
who has given me this moment in time, and it is to you
that I give my Eternal Thanks . . .

Thanks I give for a mothers most precious gift an unbreakable bond that only God himself can remove or lift, For future lessons in life I have yet to learn . . . I can only hope that a gift, a gift of love such as this I will be able to one day return . . . .

A mothers gift is most precious indeed . . .
Carolyn, this is what you have given to me . . . .

A Mothers' Love

Countless tears you have shed, sacrifices you've made
untold, yet not a sound do we hear nor complaint will
be stated cause when a hard decision came up you made
it and stood by it in spite of it all . . .

A faithful and proud woman you are and it shows
through, you've earned this pride despite what life's
trials has brought to you, not one scream or shout in
order to get a job done, no that uncouth behavior is just
not you, always getting your point across and that is
the honest to Gods truth . . .

From all the years I've come to know and learn the
woman that you are, it is always showing faith that God
is in your heart and will never leave but always pull you
through, You have been blessed with Gods own grace
as this is what he has placed within you for the world to
see and with all this being said . . . .

Jeanette your acceptance has
meant the world to me . . .

The Legacy of A Matriarch

They say the eyes are the window to the soul and if
you look into her eyes there will be stories untold, all
the heartache and pain she's been through all for her
children, that's all of you . . .

She can tell you about struggles, she can tell you about
strife and about all the horrible stories she's been
through in her life, she can tell you about the beginning
and the ending from whence you came such is the
legacy that she brings . . . .

She can tell you about all the sorrow that life can bring,
she can show you your ups from your downs and how
to turn your life around, all this is just a mere part of
the legacy she continues to give from the heart, you can
look into her eyes and see all the sacrifices that she has
made time after time for all of you including me . . .

Sacrifices that came at such a great cost but she doesn't feel the loss at all, see she has given you such a wondrous gift that is a legacy no one can lift, it can't be bought or stolen, it can't be battered or bruised and it can only be passed on and not passed through . . .
This moment in time is for all to stop and think where would you be today if she hadn't gone through all those things . . . .

This wondrous woman God made, this tower of strength and pride, wisdom that is overflowing as she passes it down through time, this vision of beauty you see before your very eyes, this is a woman of passion, and loyalty untold that boldly paved the way for you all to go . . .

All this embodies Cora Lee Dement for she is the Legacy of a Matriarch that God has sent

My Son, My blessing

It seems that you've been with me for just a little while and the years have flown by, faster than I ever thought they would and now you stand before me almost a man, I can see how truly blessed I have been for the Lord to grant me such a wondrous gift . . .

Only God above knows how much you mean to me, have been my sunshine when I could only see the rain, your smiles shine through the darkness and bring me to the light again, I made a vow to myself the day you were born to never let you come to any kind of harm, for this is the devils world we are living in and it has every kind of imaginable sin . . .

As I made my vow to you and I'd stake my life on this, if you were ever taken unjustly from me the devil would have one very pissed off mother he'd have to deal with . . . From the bottom of my heart to the very depths of my soul, I thank the Lord for a son like you De'Angeleo and every trial that you've put me through . . . Yes I know they were only little blessings in disguise . . .

Within you I clearly see . . . Loyalty that knows no bonds, Intelligence that stretches for miles around, Strength of character that is forged in steel that ensures you will never bend to someone else's will, All this I see wrapped in a Heart of Gold . . . . This is the son of Eighteen years I have come to know . . .

Smiles, tears, laughter and yes heartache and pain I chant this to the Lord every night when I pray . . . .

Thank you Lord for my child, Thanks for Blessing me . . . With a love that Death can't steal

Your Mother ~ Angel~

My Child, My Gift

Put your arms around me child just like you use to do
and with each passing year you get a little Older but
you will always be mommies baby boo . . .

My child, my child don't you fret or cry just tell
Momma what's wrong and dry these tears from your
eyes, I know I make you mad sometimes and honey
believe me your feelings, they do show . . .

I will always try to be around in your time of need, but
believe me that when I can't, know that I love you and
you are precious to me . . .

When I loose my patience with you and, at times it seems overboard and mean, I later apologize because I know that once in a while that wasn't right, it's only because I want you to achieve everything in your dreams . . .

My child Toriano I love you so, but as you grow I must keep in mind that you were only lent to me and one day I must set you free . . .

With a love Everlasting—
YourMother ~Angel~

Daughter of My Heart

It was eighteen ears ago, the day we met and as a child
you touched a part of me that few others could reach,
as if the Lord had given you a light so that darkness in
others you could breach, it was then you became the
daughter of my heart
and also captured a piece of my soul . . .

Daughter of my heart, captive of my soul, know that
the Lord gave you this light and it gives you total
control of your life, in him there is nothing you cannot
do making you the leader you are today, inspiring
others to be their best and do all they can do, all the
while showing them his way, this is what you were
meant to do, allowing the light that resides within you
to shine through . . .

As a young woman there will be trials and tribulations
that will be sent your way, there will also be hard
decisions that you will someday have to make,
remember these are tests that we all must face and
know that the Lord is thy comfort and will give you
strength and fortitude to make it through . . .
just remember even in the darkness his light lill shine
as it is a integral part of you

Kind, Intelligent, God fearing, and what a Beautiful
child of God you are, Tarasae you will forever
be . . .
The Daughter of My Heart

Illusions of Love Lost

Love Gone Cold

Said your love was forever true, yet look how I've just found you, here taking the cowards way out, packing your stuff, you and she about to sneak out the house . . . while I' was at work no less . . . .

I left this morning you were alone saying you needed to stay home, well it's clear to see you and she were not expecting me to come home and check on you a little early . . . Standing in the bedroom door, my blood ran cold, my heart hit the floor . . .

I stand and stare kinda in a daze not realizing the look of murderous rage that is on my face, no this isn't happening I say to myself, you and she no, no this cannot be ! I look from you to her and ask why, my best friend or so I thought . . . why

I wasn't supposed to find out this way and you never wanted to cause me this pain, or so you say, but she is the one you now love . . .

I guess the signs were there all along self denial is a hard pill to swallow . . . .

A love gone cold is all I have left to show . . . . trust is
at times
such
a
dirty
word . . . .

A Lonely Road

Why do I walk this road alone I often wonder why, why
I walk this road of memories all of you and I . . .

I wonder at times asking myself, if we could start again,
if things could have been different . . . . I wonder why
every now and then . . .

People see me walk down this road and ask me why,
why do I think of memories that will only make me
cry . . . . I try to hide the hurt in my eyes . . . But it's
just too much to pretend that things are like they use to
be back then . . .

Why do I take that walk, that walk back down memory
lane, when you won't be there to meet me and it's hard
to stand the pain . . .

The answer is I only wish you could forgive the things
that were said, things that I did . . . when getting back
at you only caused me pain in the end . . . .

Why do I walk this road alone when Thinking back I
know two wrongs don't make a right and at times even
I wonder why I walk this road of memories that
I can not
seem
to
let
die . . .

Guilty Of Love

Guilty your Honor pass sentence upon me, the crime
that was committed ; stealing a love not meant to be,
this weary heart heard my conscious say . . .
"Don't trust a cheater who just wants to play, in the end
your heart will only pay" . . . .

Yes I heard all the words, yet thought nothing of
price, gave up all my self respect and ignored all good
advice, never thinking that in the end . . . after we were
lovers . . .
we could never be friends . . .

He was such a good actor, play acting his part, that
even though I set him free . . . he still has my heart . . . .

Took a love that God forbade and paid the price with
a broken heart and a empty soul as the highest of
spades . . .

Think before you act and you'll end up happier,
especially
with God
on your side

Just an Illusion

Why did I have to love him, how did I stand the pain,
he swore to me he was being faithful but then the
rumors would start
all over again . . .

My friends tell me they see him out on the town, they
think they're being supportive but the news just brings
me down . . .

Looking at old pictures of a face I use to kiss, now lines
of sorrow and tear stained traces are a legacy that no
one
can seem to lift . . .

Each time he left me a part of me slowly died, after
so many shared experiences it was hard to break the
ties . . .

Evidence just kept mounting up that this time he'd
gone to far, the calls at all hours of the night and the
pictures in his car . . .

My need for him just eroded, when it was clear to me
that we were not worth fighting for and his needs
mattered more, now I just let him go although it makes
me sad . . .

I now realize I can't keep a love
I never
really
had . . .

Happy to Let Em' Go

Such a fool not to see it coming, you always had one
foot out the door, this time you say it really is over so
do me a favor and just go cause you can't
hurt me
anymore . . . .
Go ahead and try to live the good life, but don't come
back to me saying your sorry, Im not the same naive
fool that I use to be . . . .

Bye-Bye hope you have a good life, see you later I don't
hate you, but you say you'll see me around . . .

Not if I see
you
first . . .

Honesty

I was going to tell you the truth
but that was before I found out how much I really cared
about you . . . .

Be honest, if I had told you the truth from the start
you would have broken this young girls heart, so I lied
instead . . .

Lying to you was wrong but I want to try to explain,
the depth of my feelings and a little of my pain . . . .

I wanted to tell you and Only God knows how much,
but I knew if I did you would tell me it was over, before
we could even begin, so once again . . .

I lied . . .

Looking back back I must have been a little out of my head as this didn't serve the purpose I had in my mind,

Our bind wasn't strong enough to stand against the pressure and the toll it took on a man's pride, and it was that pride that could not handle the truth in it's rarest form

Didn't even try to understand my reasons why I did what I did, just to busy listening to the unsolicited advice of your friends, to busy to be your own man that you couldn't handle the truth in
the
end . . .

Broken Heart

Broke his heart is what I did, he just would not
accept that I just wanted to be his friend, I thought
he understood how I felt but when he told me that he
loved me, it hit me
below the belt . . .

When he finally came around, I made him see that a
relationship was something that at that time we didn't
need . . .

He could have taken that, but no he wanted more,
knowing that I couldn't give it so what hell did he keep
coming
around me for . . .

Friendship was all I had to offer and Im sorry to say he
still wanted more so I had to end a friendship that took
so long to build . . .
I knew we could go
no
farther . . .

A Haunting Decision

I wouldn't go that far with you, there was always
something more important I just had to do, telling you
back then I loved you but I wasn't ready for a serious
relationship
yet . . .

You waited for me for such a long while, you wanted
marriage, you wanted a child, wanting too much too
soon, to me we were children ourselves back then . . .

I wouldn't go that far with you, I had dreams to fulfill
things to important for me to ignore,
years went by and yes I did succeed but you got tired of
waiting and said you that you would always love me but
would wait no more and that it was over . . .

I saw you the other day looking so happy and content,
me on the other hand successful but alone and
miserable, things that were once so important don't
seem so anymore, I now ask myself why couldn't that
be me, all because I wouldn't take that chance with
you . . .

I stand by my decision and place no blame on you as
I know it was my fault, but at what cost that is the
question that now
haunts me . . .

A found love that is
forever
lost . . .

Hurting

It hurts when it's over, so hard to say good-bye, the
ending of a relationship, is so hard to break the ties . . .

Still thinking of you, but it hurts so much, especially
when thinking of all the nights sitting there waiting for
your call, never to receive one at all, not even a letter in
the mail to say stop waiting
go to hell . . .

You seem to forget you're no longer in a relationship,
you go around in a daze because the memories are just
like yesterday It hurts when it's
over . . .

It hurts so much, you just can't seem to forget as
the memories cling to your subconscious going back
in time when that person you still think of as 'mine'
mainly it hurts when it's over cause its
hard to say
good-bye . . .

A Women's Worth

Behind Closed Doors

He was always the perfect gentleman when out in the
public eye, always calm, cool and collected, he was so
good an actor that not even close friends and family
knew what he was really like . . . behind closed doors

A liar, a cheat, but always he was discreet, you'd never
know about his many affairs in, London, Rome, and
even Spain his affairs went on and on, his wife knew but
no one would think it caused her great pain . . .

Oh he beat her down many a day, but it wasn't the kind
of physical abuse, oh no those wounds they go away, it
was the mental abuse that she took day after day, those
are the kind of wounds that stay . . . stay behind closed
doors . . .

She left him . . . once, but she went back I guess she
didn't know where to go or what else to do so she takes
the affairs and mental abuse in stride taking comfort
and pride that no one knows what goes on . . .

Behind her closed doors

Foolish Pride

Hateful words, obscenities all said in a moment of raging passion, both trying to hide the pain they inflict upon each other . . . thats not love, thats pride, foolish, foolish pride . . .

He beats on her and everyone knows it, they've even called the police a time or two but every time they came she said "get offa my porch this ain't nobody's business! but me and mines!" even though she had a busted lip and two black eyes . . . I say to her and myself it ain't you business girl, it's your foolish pride . . .

She's finally left him, and he promised her one day she'd pay, she laughed it off and didn't go to the police like everyone told her, oh no and besides she thought people need to mind their own damned business anyway . . . once again foolish pride is what she's got that's what I say . . .

He stalked her for months on end and the day came
that he made good on his promise, he almost beat her
to death and left their two children alone in this world
without a mother . . .

Now she's learned her lesson but she learned it the
hard way . . .

Never let pride, foolish pride get in the way when help
is just
a call away . . .

Self Deception

Knowing the truth yet . . . still trying to hide, thinking
everything will be alright . . .
Mixed up in past pain, feeling it today as if it just
happened yesterday, instead of the years it has taken to
bring you to this boiling point, convinced that the pain
has been long buried in the past where it belongs . . .
Yet in reality you never let it go . . . Still think its ok?

Think again . . . Sticking your head in the sand when
you need to be taking a stand for all the wrongs that
you've accepted for so long,
smiling all the while your heart is breaking, feeling
dead, empty inside, yet you tell anyone who will listen
that everything is ok, it's alright, and then go home to
let the dam burst . . . .

Self-deception is a deadly weapon that only hurts the
person that wields it,
and that's . . .

YOU . . .

Know Thy Self

Take a look inside yourself and tell me what you see,
are you a wise and solid soul who stands tall and strong
when faced with adversity, or will you run like a coward
running from
its foe . . . .

Look at yourself and go very, very deep inside, do you
really know yourself?, do you always tell the truth or
sometimes lie? trying to convince everyone including
yourself that all you really did was tell a
small
white
lie . . .

There are rules to follow in order to have
a truthful, and honest
soul searching mission . . .

Must first be true to you, and only you before
attempting this with someone else, always know
your weakness and limitations in each and every
situation . . . .

Be loyal and steadfast in your beliefs, following your intuition, instinct and you will almost never go
wrong . . .

Take a look in the mirror, what do you see, is this the person that is filled with self confidence? proud of what you are today, looking forward to tomorrow? or are you a person full of self doubt and loathing? mad at the world for the mess you've made
of your
life?

Are you embittered by the harsh realities of what is going on in todays world and
your part in it?

Shakespeare said it best "the world is a stage and we mere actors playing parts" ask yourself if you were given is the part you want to play for the rest of your life as you only live once
and
then you die . . .

Look inside before you judge anyone else, all I ask is that you look inside and see if to you there is honesty, integrity, and truth because when searching inside you'll need to be careful and sure that you want to find the truth, in some cases you might find that you are the person you hate the
most . . . .

So what do you see . . .

Forgiveness

It is said that we should ourselves forgive 70x7 in a day
yet I have to ask after this is done will it take the pain
away . . .

The humiliation in knowing that you have accepted the
lies, physical and emotional pains as well as defeat, yet
all this should be in the past, it is for these things that
you forgive but how long will the forgiveness last, that
is what I must ask . . .

To reach for a hand to find that you have yet again
been left behind, feeling nothing but air, to forgive one
more time with these feelings of despair . . . pondering
upon thing such as this and It must be said, it's as if
something is amiss something that is just out of your
reach . . .

Oh now you get it, now You see . . . .
You must forgive yourself before
You can do so for anyone else . . . .

Hmmmm . . .
Where
to
start . . .

J'am, J see, J know

Beautiful, intelligent, with a witty sense of humor, I
also come in many different hues the most unpopular
one
being black . . .

Like most of us I knew only a little of my true heritage,
unable to pin down my forefathers in the past, but
I can and will tell you what is in the future of all
African Americans if we do not continue to teach each
generation the truths of Unity and Strength we all
should hold dear in
our hearts . . . .

I see uncle toms kissing up, moving in the wrong
direction denying they're true heritage trying to be
something
they are not . . .

More and more of our brothers and sisters are stealing
from each other, killing each other, incarcerated for
crimes committed
and not . . .

In general I see a heritage being destroyed and at this
pace will most definitely not survive becoming extinct
like so many before . . .

I know how to take all this in stride as I said beautiful,
intelligent, and learning how to keep my heritage
alive . . .

Standing Tall,
Standing Proud

Hold your hear up girl, stand and walk real proud don't
you ever let anybody degrade or put you down . . .

You need to see you are the vessel and God is your
guide and if allowed to lead the way for you, nobody
but nobody can interrupt the flow of your stride . . .

Stand tall, stand proud as you don't have anything to
hide . . .

People may laugh and snicker when you walk across the
room, don't pay any attention to those immature fools,
instead . . .

Stand tall, Stand proud,
you see God is watching over
you . . .

Trust

Trust isn't something that you can buy, it's a feeling
that comes from deep inside, this is what I feel for you
and I just hope you feel the same way too . . .

If you don't feel it towards me then I must ask, what do
you actually feel for me . . . this is how I feel inside and
when I tell you this trust is what I'am abiding by in my
love for you . . .
I trust you with my heart, my soul I trust you to at
times be in control totally, and I hope you can feel the
same with me, this is what I have in my heart for you
and I pray that you feel this way too . . .

I now know, I must first trust myself before I can
demand this from
someone else . . .

Trust . . . Can you . . .

Searching for Love

Lies, deceit, dishonesty, I wonder is there any love left
out there
for me . . .

If I ever find love I would want a mutual respect,
someone that won't look down
on me because of all
my deficiencies . . .

For without trust, honesty, and respect a relationship
is dead, so if no one has these things what part besides
sex
do they have left . . .

Maybe what I want is asking for too much, but surely
you can't shoot a dreamer for merely dreaming too
much . . .

For I won't settle for anything less . . .
Searching for love,
is there any
left . . .

Life's Lessons and Trials

Past, Present, and Future

Call me young and even wet behind the ears but I know
a lot about the suffering we have endured throughout
the years . . .

They call this the land of the free and home of the
brave, yet they don't really know how dearly we have
all paid, the price that was paid in blood, sweat, and a
hell of a lot of tears all this we have shed throughout
the years . . . .

We all have been bought and at sometime or another
broken, we have been chained and bound, beat up and
put down, but our spirits have never and will never be
yours to keep as a token, you may break my heart . . . .
but my spirit will never
be broken . . .

America's Shame

A past that lies in slavery, and not speaking out
against the atrocities committed by one race against
another . . . .

Shame that lies in pretending an ignorance of it's
past sins, the knowledge is there for them to seek and
try to learn from their mistakes yet it stays in the
closet blatantly ignored, unlearned and unheeded . . .
America's shame lies in ignorance . . .

Allowing select groups to preach messages of hate,
messages which lead to unspeakable actions against
another racially selected group of people, or should I
say targeted group or groups of people . . .

Allowing select groups to take our Freedom of Speech
too damn far . . . America's shame lies in Tolerance . . .

How does America's various shames affect you? If you
think it doesn't you are a fool . . . .

America's shame . . . . Not having enough forethought
regarding the people's future . . .

America's shame . . . . Not having any . . . . at all . . . .

My shame Vs My Pride

I did not want to learn the truth, the truth about me
and also about you . . . My shame lay in being ashamed
to
be black . . .

My shame was a heritage and a culture older then the
bible, it taught the truth and knew many rivals, my
shame was ignorance and the tolerance of so many
lives wasted and taken away for such a
long time . . . .

Believing all the lies that were taught about my people,
taught by people who's intent was twisted with hatred
and every kind of evil . . . My shame lay in not knowing
the Truth . . . .

My shame . . . Being ashamed that my ancestors came
over here on slave ships, they came here in shackles and
were beaten down with horse whips . . .

My shame lies in not hearing their cries for help,
America's shame lies in hearing yet ignoring their cries,
you heard them, yet you still enslaved their lives . . .
A shame indeed

Now My pride, my pride lies in knowing the truth, the
truth about me and about you, My pride lies in having a
heritage and culture of people who were just . . .
to strong . . .
to die . . . .

My pride lies in NOT being ashamed to be
ME
anymore . . . .

Judgment . . . Who Are You

You don't know a thing about me, yet you try to judge me as if I m not good enough to be a part of the human race,

You try to act as if my color doesn't matter, but I can see the difference when I glance at the disdainful expression that looks as if it has been permanently etched upon your face . . . .

Who are you to judge me and behind my back call me names? It doesn't change my color as you can it is here to stay . . . .

Every race is different so who are you to judge Me or anyone else and find them lacking? It only shows how truly ignorant you are . . .

Judging anyone by looks and color alone is a very shallow thing to do, and you just never know what someone else may be thinking about you . . .

Judgement . . . .
Race Part 2

Race . . . We come in all shapes, sizes, and colors
evidently God wanted it this way, so why waste time
hating each other when it only brings bitterness
and pain . . . .?

It was written . . . For the measure that you judge you
too will be judged with seven times that measure, that
is in a
universal sense . . . .

Race . . . . You are apart of one and it's just to bad you
see, for even though you may hate my guts you are a
part of me . . . How the Hell is that you may say . . . .

I'll gladly tell you why . . . Well we are ALL a part of
the Human race therefore we are all connected by the
one Supreme being and only he can judge, for he judges
by your hearts content not by the color
of your skin . . .

You may still try to judge me, however I will not do the
same, you see its not in my nature, Im not like that, so
I refuse to be anything like you, for anyone who judges
by looks and the color of ones skin alone are to be
labeled as fools . . .

I guess you will be the one held unworthy in the end
hmmm . . . .

So I ask again and again
Who are you? . . .

Life Pulls No Punches

Go up two steps, they knock you down but don't just
sit there and fret and frown cause you know that's what
they want you to do, take my advice don't sit there
looking around like a fool who hasn't a clue of what to
do . . .

Common sense tells us that when we fall down or
someone knocks us down a peg or two, just get right
back up . . . swinging if you have to . . .

Life's to hard for the weak and weary and as they say
only the strong survive . . . Not knowing that the weak
have a different kind of strength and mentality that
they have hidden deep inside . . .

Who knows when the guard is dropped and and the
chips are down and if given half a chance you just
might be surprised at who's on top in the end . . .

Drug Dealer

Think you're the ghetto healer, selling your
non-prescriptive drugs, your people are dying in the
street without enough food to eat and you think your
showing them
some love . . .

I bet you think you happy now, while you're selling that
stuff your people are dying, you gonna go to jail and
your Momma's gonna be crying, then where you
gonna be . . .

Think you bad with all that money, think you cute in
all those expensive clothes, oh yeah you popular in the
hood driving that fancy new car, but let me tell you
something . . . . your friends ain't who you think
they are . . . .

Sold you out for a bag of dope and now you in jail
refusing to tell without an ounce of hope, Drug
dealer . . . Mr. Drug dealer ! ahem . . .
Where are your friends and
money now . . . .?

Isn't It Ironic

You look at a bum sitting in a corner across the street,
you shake your head and walk pass not giving a second
thought about them or lending a helping hand . . . a
month or two later that bum is you . . . lend a helping
hand if you can even if you don't have to . . .

Someone being raped in the middle of a park, you hear
it but don't see it, go get help or lend a hand don't just
stand around and criticize wondering what in the hell
they were doing in a park at that time of night, so you
ignore it, saying that has nothing to do with you . . .
not knowing that was someone you knew . . . . isn't it
ironic

Some people born with money just don't have a clue
of what people without it, go through, so they act like
they're better then me and you, they snub you and have
the nerve to treat you like dirt . . .

Later you see them again and they're filling out a
application at the same place of employment as you . . .

Isn't it Ironic

Mirror Image

What even the poorest man in the world doesn't know is that for some of the richest men their money is mostly for show, it brings but a brief happiness, for what legacy does he have left except money to leave for time moves on and so do memories . . .

The poor man knows that his time on this earth has a limit and true happiness catches only a few, while the rich man has briefly glimpsed happiness and now thinks that he can live forever if he wants to . . . .

Envy, resentment, bitterness, and a world weary cynicism they have for the other goes bone deep, they each have stayed up many a night because they can't seem to sleep . . . each wanting what the other has

They have something in common, each search for
true happiness, contentment, and maybe even peace,
peace from the war raging inside themselves for such
a long time, not knowing that self acceptance, true self
acceptance and all that is good comes from within and
this can only happen if they accept God in their life as a
mentor well as a friend

This is what is needed, yet of this they haven't a
clue . . . They have a mirror image, look in the mirror
and see if the face on the other side is you . . .

A Heavy Load

Lord there is something heavy that is laying on my heart, someone needs prayer and I don't know where to start . . . .

Lord how do I reach a person who has a hardened heart? I'm praying to you as it seems that I've had a slow start . . . .

The world has beaten bitterness into whom I'm trying to reach, and now Lord I feel ready finally for the patience that you've so long to me been trying to teach . . .

Lord, I know you hear me so I'll just wait hopefully in peace, because this is a heavy load that I know that one day off my shoulders you will release . . .

A Letter to a Drug Addict

Can you hear my cries, can you feel the pain, its as if I
have lost you all over again . . . the first time I lost you
it was to the drugs, you lied to me, stole from me, you
threw away
my love . . .

This time you've gone away paying societies price, I
know it's the hardest thing for you to do, but I know it
will
be alright . . .

Can you hear what I'm saying? if not read between the
lines, if you think that I've left you or that I no longer
love you then you must be deaf, dumb, and blind . . .

I'll always be there for you from now until eternity, and
if you're ever feeling down and lonely just drop me line
and then you'll see just how loyal, loving and honest I
can be . . .

I want you back, yet I
have to wonder
if you can
hear
me . . .

Searching for Redemption

Birth was given to you years ago and now the pain and
heartache is what I can't take anymore . . .

The past five years of your life ain't done nothing but
gone down the drain, and you use to have such a good
head on your shoulders, yet again the drugs have done
a hell of a job on your brain . . .

Tell me why, why did you make the choice to go down
that road, when everyone told you that it wasn't the
right
way to go . . .

I guess hit after hit you were searching for that same
high, the very high that hit you so good the first time
you almost died, what a hard road to take while already
living a lie . . .
Could it be true, that you really have changed, I'm
sitting here praying for you cause if so the choice you
made was right . . .

Although I'm proud of you, this must be said I don't
trust you at this time as the trust was thrown away
with the lying, cheating, and stealing you did to me and
others
day after day . . .

I won't give my trust as easily as I did before cause it
now must be earned, but I will continue to give freely
what I can, and that is the unconditional love that will
allow you to one day be a great man . . .

This road you have taken won't be easy, it will probably
be the hardest thing you have to do, as when searching
for redemption you finally realize that the world doesn't
revolve
around . . . .

You

Worthy . . . Or Not . . .

Fancy cars, diamond rings, and designer clothes, yes all
these are very expensive things, things that can give
the appearance of prestige, wealth, fortune and fame . . .
sometimes to the very people who can and will only
give lip service to my name . . .

They give to charities from pockets that deep some
without a second thought to the cause if you know
what I mean, yet they say they know me . . . if not by
heart . . .
then certainly by
deeds

Understanding not, that it is not money, but simply
giving from the heart, thats worth its weight in
gold . . .

Yet I wonder when they finally realize this, will it be
too late to save their souls? . . .

Worthy or Not . . .
Only
God
Knows . . .

Contemplation

The show must go on that's what they say I must do,
but do they know how hard going on is, that's the
question
I am now asking you

They say just keep going on, don't think just do, if only
they knew even half of what was going on inside of my
head,
Im telling you . . .

So I put on a smile, joke around a bit, all the while
trying to forget what's going on in my life for a minute,
yet . . .

They don't feel my pain, and don't see my tears, or
know the things I have had to endure over the past few
months or years, so how can they judge for me
if I can go on
or
not . . .

Yet you, your self could not see what was before your own eyes, not paying attention to the smile that doesn't quite reach my eyes, or see that Im just a shadow of my former self, having yet to realize that I am contemplating . . .

The taking of my own life, wanting to give up and just say I quit !!
Would that mean I am weak in your eyes
and can't
handle
it . . .

Is it Worth It

I've often thought about committing suicide, although
that is not the way I ever thought I would want to die,
is it worth it . . .

Is it worth it . . . the struggle, the strife just wanting to
give it all up, and walk away from my life . . . I seem to
be asking myself this question a lot lately . . .

The pain and the problems of my life at times seem
to much to bear, and too high a price to pay so I tell
myself that no one cares so why should
I then I think life just isn't fair . . .
thats
why . . .

I now know it is not even though the pain and pressure
of this world I can not seem to stop . . .

While the pain will not go away the show must go on
with the pain . . .
or
Not . . .

Essence of Life

Smiles go with laughter as the tears often mingled
in pain, joy is followed by sadness, like sunshine is
followed by the rain, the skies are mostly clear and
blue yet they too hold mysteries, as the clouds fold over
the crystalized blueness to leave the sky in a murky
existence
why is this . . .

Relationships and emotions are sometimes like this
never quite knowing what will happen next trying to
take two days at a time instead of the one we know we
must take to move on to the next level . . .

Joy and pain, darkness and light, faith mixed with hope,
sorrow mixed with despair, love and hate, all in the
same
heart . . .

How do you know you love someone with all these
emotions swirling around, waiting to erupt like a
volcano in the right place,
yet erupting
at the
wrong
time . . . .

Random Thoughts

Some think the world
revolves around revolution, some even say that science
is the solution, I say turn to God and clear your mind
of
all that pollution . . .

Some think the end is coming soon and one day we will
be able to live on other planets even the moon, I have
the greatest doubts of this being true, you see even
with all this science and technology we still have to
turn to God if you want to be free of this world and
its hypocrisies . . .

Some build grand churches yet fill them with fools, the
same fools that think they have the right to judge me
and you, knowing full well that just because some don't
go to church doesn't mean that in their life
God doesn't work . . .

Some say that the riches of this world have nothing to
offer and with those few I do agree, you see to me they
are the
wise ones
indeed . . .

Pondering Questions

How do you reach people who don't to be reached,
how can a preacher speak to those who don't want to
hear him preach? how does one know that good will
eventually triumph over evil? all these questions are
part of the game, the game of who will
follow the leader . . .

How do you know the difference between the truth and
a lie, how do you know that you were not promised to
live, but you have a guarantee that one day you will
surely die . . .

How do you calculate how high an eagle flies, how do
scientists know that when one species cease to exist
another triumphs due to its will to survive . . .

How do we know that the end is near, and that when
we pray Jesus lends us his never ending ear . . .

Look into your heart for the answers lie within, and if
you are not a fool all that I have said will to you make
sense . . .

This Too Shall Pass

The shallow dead look in your eyes tells me that you
have given up on life, remember things are never as bad
as they seem, for this too shall pass don't give up
on me . . .

Greed, bigotry, anger, and hatred, the first in the name
of money, the second in the name of ignorance and
stupidity, the third stems from a well that runs deep
within, the fourth leads to wicked thoughts and deeds,
this to shall pass soon enough you'll see, all you have to
do is give your life, mind, body, and soul
to me . . .

Pain, and grief are not at times what they seem, you see
you can turn the pain around and the grief gives you
the inner strength you need to bring your problems
to me . . .

If you think that you still cannot cope remember these
things too shall pass and this should give you sufficient
hope . . .

Humorous

Momma Knows

You think I don't what goes on behind your bedroom
doors, or how you end up off your bed with a blanket
on the floor, and what about the time you tried to sneak
out the house to play Dr. with the little girl next
door . . .

Oh, and all the times you put cookies in the cart when
we went to the grocery store, remember even when you
think my back is turned Momma always
knows . . .

Dinner time, we're all at the table waiting for you
to say grace, and you sneak a piece of candy in your
mouth then try to hide your face, you thought I wasn't
looking and that just goes to show, that even when you
think I don't
Momma
always
knows . . .

Subject: Men . . .

There are men you absolutely love, some men you love
to hate, the subject of men is kind of hard to debate,
some as you know like to beat you down, while still
yet others like to try and put you down whenever your
friends
are around . . .

They like to put in their place, while still yet others will
get embarrassed and try to slap you in the face, men
some are good some are bad, at times while you find
you're with one often wishing for a man you know you
cant have . . .
Men . . .

Some men you love, some men you leave and some men
are just to hard to believe . . . .
Men . . .

Loves Price

You can play the game of love, but even in love there is
a price, a price that everyone must pay at least once in
their life . . .

Some pay a little more, some pay less the price of true
love is a high one as Im sure you've already
guessed . . .

Saying Good-Bye

A Broken Promise

A heart makes a promise before it fades away, an augury
of fulling love and then the heart dies . . .

Some hearts open slowly, some hearts may not open at
all, and if love comes too early it could die in the cold of
a
wintery fall . . .

Late love is like a flower with love vows not always
spoken, between the loves and hates a promise might be
broken . . .

Take the love that you have today and cherish it in a
most sacred way, for you'll never know when or why a
promise will be broken or a loved one
will
die . . .

My Love, My Loss

My heart cries, my soul bleeds, as I am down on bended
knee, praying that the light continues to shine as I
think in my mind of you and all the laughs, smiles,
heartache and tears that will be
no more . . .

All the rough lessons I've learned and had to endure
through my few years here in a sometimes cold and
cruel
world . . .

Through all the hurts and the pain there is one thing
that remains constant, it has and will never change . . .

The strength that God gives is what keeps us sane,
along with his promise that you and I will one day meet
again . . .

Reminding myself that it is in the darkest hours that he
carries his children through the pain, knowing he will
bring you into his light once more is what keeps my
faith strong and helps me sleep
at night . . .

Forget Not

Forget me not for I can never forget you, see when I
left this world a piece of you with me T took too, my
father called me home that day, and I had to answer his
call, now I want you to understand that doing this was
no hardship
at all . . .

When the Lord reached out I gladly took his hand for
the for the pains of this world I could no longer stand,
now I know it will be hard, but you must let me go for
it's tearing me apart to see you
suffer
so . . .

Look for the memories that now lay in the past for
these are the memories which will forever last, if only
you decide to move forward and learn to relinquish and
not cling to the
past . . .

Forget not the promise that Lord has made "come to me all who are heavy laden and I will give you rest . . .

For the ones who now lay at rest are with God as they have passed their final test, forget not the good times that you had to share for they will see you through even the hardest seasons of the year . . .

Please forget not but let me go . . .

Had I Only Known

If only I had known that this was good-bye, it would
have made it easier and I wouldn't sit here and
cry . . .

I would have taken down all the good times that we had
to share, but I didn't and now the memories are almost
too much
to bare . . . .

Had I known that this was the end, I would have said I
loved you a lot more often . . .

It came up so suddenly first you were here with me and
then like a thief in the night, almost like a flash of light
then you were
just gone . . .

If only I had known all the would haves, could haves,
should haves won't change the past, I would have left
all harsh words unsaid, left them alone rolling around
in my head, but now its to late because now
your gone,
just
gone . . .

Always think before you speak, you never know if those
will be the last words your loved one will
hear . . .